T0149988

Vintage
Wisdom

Published by Polaris
an imprint of
North Star Press of St. Cloud Inc.

Vintage Wisdom

A COLLECTION OF REFLECTIONS,
QUOTES, AND BELIEFS
FROM SPECIAL FRIENDS

Compiled by:
Jim Secord

"Wisdom is nothing but a preparation of the soul, a capacity, a secret art of thinking, feeling and breathing thoughts of unity at every moment of life"

-Hermann Hesse

My very dear friends,

This is *your* book! Whatever you wrote, whomever you may have quoted, whatever you wanted to express, however you wanted your thoughts to be seen or heard in this little book, you gave me and others an exceptional gift. Thank you.

Your wisdom came in many flavors, indeed. To some of you it was a special writing from an author you admired or inspired you. For others of you, it was a word or only a sentence. And in a number of cases, several of you retrieved memories of stories and of your life's truths.

For some of you, your responses were immediate, while others *suffered* through the exercise. And one of you very wise and talented people even wrote this to accompany your piece: "You probably have no idea how difficult it is for me to set down a few 'words of wisdom' without the fluttering of little devils around my head accusing me of arrogance and preaching, prating and sanctimoniousness! I tie myself in knots." Such honesty!

For me, *all* of your responses are wonderful, most simply because they are from you. They are what you took time to send, at that given time, when you penned your words, typed a letter, or hit the send button on your computer or smartphone. No one else did this for you, they were all yours. Whether your contributions were short, long, or quotes, they are each profound in their own unique way, all individual gifts to me and the other writers.

In thinking back to my original idea and motivation for requesting your words, perhaps it may have been my subliminal objective to challenge all of you to reflect on your values, to dig a bit deeper than what you might normally do, as to what really is important at this stage of your being, and to have the courage to bring that forward for the rest of us to witness. Just maybe, that was a driver for my request.

I've had until now the exclusive benefit of reading and rereading all of your contributions. I've lived with some of them for several months, while I received others more recently. In the preparation for this book, I've personally typed your responses a minimum of two times, and others, three or four.

One of my goals of this intensive preparation, in the rereading and retyping, was to *feel* you, to be in proximity and union with you as if I were writing your piece myself. It is because of this that I have fallen in love with what you sent to me.

With that in mind, I would like to be bold in suggesting that you also search out for yourself the hiddenness of these writings. Not all, of course, but those that initially speak to you as they have to me. And should one or two especially capture you, and you want to express it to the writer, send me an email and I will pass your thoughts on to them.

So now you have the result of your work. May you be as thankful to yourselves for contributing your wisdom as I have been in receiving it. As said at the beginning of this overture, this is your book! May it bring you pleasure and well deserved satisfaction for having participated.

With gratitude and love,
Jim S.

P.S. If you would like to contact me, please email me here: jimsecord36@gmail.com

Origin, content,
and editing of this book

I have been blessed with many exceptional friends, more than anyone has the right
to hope for or expect. This particular exercise
brought this home to me. In the case of this
book, you have taught me much, and continue
to do so. This was not a surprise. However, I
wasn't prepared for the depth of your kindness
and generosity in responding to me as you did:
154 contributions from a request list of 167. In
addition, I received scores of accompanying
letters encouraging me about the project, along
with personal reflections and affirmations.

My intention for this book was to publish
what you sent me. No judgment, no interpret-
ing, and for sure, no exclusions. In most cases,
this intent was fulfilled. The exceptions were
when the length exceeded the guideline, or
minor editing was needed for clarity. Generally,
I attempted to communicate with several of you

before changes were made. If that did not happen, and I have altered the spirit of your contribution in any way, please accept my sincere apology.

As outlined in my original request letter, I have been purposeful in disguising the responders' full names, positions, organizations, or titles. When two or more first names were the same, I added the first initial of the second name, and in three cases, the second letter of the second name. When a response carried two names, they were both included.

All of you are my very dear friends. So much so that, although we may differ politically, religiously, and sometimes even philosophically, we have created a bond over the years that will continue. As one astute participant has written, "There are no expiration dates on long, treasured friendships, nor will there ever be."

Amen!

ORIGINAL REQUEST LETTER

Dear Friend,

Over most of my 82 years I've been blessed by having exceptional friends, colleagues, mentors, and confidantes. Some go all the way back to when I was in elementary school.

It seems lately I think more and more about the gifts you and others have brought to me, includ- ing support, deep conversation, fidelity in our relationship, and even personal sacrifice in times of need.

With that in mind, I'd like to attempt to capture, from you and others, one piece of your personal wisdom that you would be willing to pass on. Or, saying it a different way, if you could express to the world just one idea or thought above all others, what would it be? It might be one word, a sentence, or paragraph, or even longer (but perhaps limited to 150 words). Quantity of words is not the purpose of this request.

My desire is to collect the responses, yours and others' wisdom, into a book and send a copy to each of you. Each quote will only be labeled with the first name (or should there be a doubling up of names, I'll also include the last name initial).

Although this may be a simple request for some, and perhaps a bit more difficult for others, should you decide to participate (which I greatly hope you will), I'd appreciate having your words by (date). They can be returned by email or regular mail.

Thank you for having blessed me in the past, for your continued friendship, and for being part of this request.

With fond regards and appreciation,
Jim Secord

In the school of the
Lord's service, I am, as St.
Benedict reminds,
always a beginner. So
each day I begin again,
trying to pay attention to
the call to:

"Listen with the ear of
your heart."

After that, it's about
being open and willing to
share what I am able.

-Amy

Living in a world of edits, white outs, deletes, and back spaces, has led me to want several "do overs." There have been pivotal moments when I was at a place I wish I hadn't gone to, said things I wish I hadn't said, times when I wished I acted and didn't. Thinking *this is not how I saw my life*, I wanted a life full of integrity and passion, instead, I look back and think *I left a trail of messes and pain, living a life of guilt, shame and regret. Just one different choice at that exact moment and this or that would all be gone, erased, different.* Maybe. Looking back, some of those mistakes became great blessings and important lessons. No matter how hard we wish it, the past cannot be undone. It does no good to keep replaying it over in your mind, or belittling yourself for the wisdom you lacked at one time in your life. You must be ready to forgive yourself, again and again, because you will make more mistakes. Or are they mistakes at all?

-Angela

DO:

¤ Good work
¤ Lift up others
¤ Listen to understand
¤ Follow through

KNOW:

-» Who you are
-» What you believe
-» Where you want to go
-» What happens because of you
-» What you desire to be known for
-» How you want to be found
-» Who you want to find you

BE:

• Trustworthy
• Consistent
• Curious
• Likeable
• Kind
• Self-aware
• Someone people want to help twice
• Grateful

Use the word *strategy* often
and learn to play golf.

~Anne

The joy of sharing with others is a real privilege. It comes with a deep humbleness that is hard to duplicate.

4

-Babs

I have been blessed with 85 wonderful years . Yes, there have been challenges and divine transformations. I have made some mistakes, but those mistakes have made me a better person. I have strived to be a servant of divinity.

I am now moving toward that late sunset and preparing to make a journey that I have never been on before. I have been promised eternity. I am so profoundly joyful to have this knowing from my people and from other traditions. Eternity is a word, but to experience the eternity of the divine existence is beyond understanding.

I have had a lot of time to think and dream about this. There is no fear. When I was a child, my grandmother taught me about the tree. She said "What you see is supported by what you don't see." When she taught me this, I remember a grove of trees that were vibrating and strong. Those trees have withered away, but I can still see their aura and their spirit.

-Basil

As I grew up, my mother was a strong advocate of the Golden Rule, treating others as you would like to be treated, often reminding us that this was the model she wanted us, her children, to use to guide our lives. My parents exemplified the Golden Rule in their daily lives and I have tried to follow this through my vocation and avocations. I have lived a life of service and it has served me well, with no regrets. It has been my privilege to be a mentor to a number of people both during a time of post-high school teaching and as an employer. There is nothing more rewarding.

-Bea

Don't sweat the small stuff. *7*

-Beth

Two things come to mind that, when I use them, are most useful to me. They are opposite sides of the same coin:

Side one: "Pain is inevitable, but suffering is optional."
                    -Anonymous

Side two: To eliminate suffering... "If the only prayer you say in your life is thank you, that would suffice"
                    -Meister Eckhart

-Bill M.

Primum Vivere
—One day at a time.

To survive,

to wait,

to hope.

-Bill S.

Resilience is recognizing nothing in life is as bad or as good as you think it is.

Resilience is a centering that allows you to weather any situation while remaining open to great possibilities.

10

-Bill V.

Every individual is just that,
individual.

The fragrance always
stays in the hand
that gives the rose.

Don't fill in the [11]
S I L E N C E

Lighthouses blow no horns,
they only shine.

-Bill W.

Spend as much
time as you can
with children,
preferably ones
under the age
of eight.

12

-Bob B.

Whether in personal or profes-sional life, hope is necessary in overcoming adversity, but is not strong enough to realize success. This means taking action on the things you can control rather than hoping for a positive outcome. [13] This is critical. You do not need to be the person with all the right answers. Seek counsel from those with more relevant experience.

-Bob Ka

"I think that, as life is action and passion, it is required of a man that he should share the passion and action of his time at peril of being judged not to have lived."

14

~Oliver Wendell Holmes, Jr.

~Bob Ki

KEEP MOVING TO
A HIGHER LEVEL

If you always do what you always did,
you always get what you always got.

What does this mean? Most people spend
their lives doing. When they achieve a level or
an age, they ask, "What should I do next?"
That is the wrong question. The question
that should be asked is: "Who do I want to
BE?"

15

How do you find the BE? By pausing and taking the time to have reflections of the heart.
It is the heart that stores your true self and
brings out the BE. When you start living in
this space of BEingness, you will soon discover that what you are doing brings you to
the things you always wanted to have–and
you have moved to a higher level of healthy
continuing growth.

~Bob W.

Single words that I think of in others when I consider Wisdom:

Patience Respect

CHARACTER

Faith Love Family

Gratitude

16

Friendship Legacy

Teaching Sharing

Giving Smiling

Comfort

Brian

To care for another, who may not recognize or even want your love, is to love as God loves, and to know His love for you.

-Bruce D.

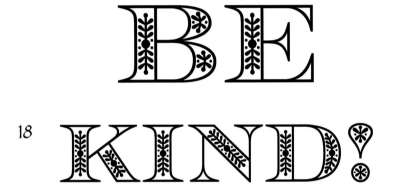

18

BE KIND!

~Bruce G

One of the biggest takeaways from my almost 40 years in business is that you are only as good as the people you have around you. If you hire good people and empower them to do their jobs, you will almost always get good results. Nowhere has this proven more true than in my latest role as Managing Director of a privately held company. We took a business that had been folded and created a new business model that included being a 100% virtual operation. The team that we hired and put in place has been tremendous at getting things done and making key decisions along the way. This allowed us to create a thriving business. The team continues to be committed to delivering many great products and services in a highly competitive industry, all while working from home.

-Bryan

In 1991, at the age of 55, I moved from Pennsylvania to Minnesota. Since living in Minnesota, I have experienced two important connections with two very special people.

First, in the 1990's, a new friend started inviting us to his annual Thanksgiving dinners. These get-togethers were memorable because of the 6 ethnic groups of people that were always invited.

The second connection was in 1997, when I was invited to another friend's Lakota Ceremonies at Pine Ridge, South Dakota. This relationship lasted over 22 years.

Why have these two people made such an impression on me? Even though they came from two different cultures, they always treat every person they meet with equal respect and dignity.

~Bud

One cannot do better in life

Than to be considered by others

To be a person of high integrity

~Burt

The only **REAL** time is the **present moment.** Embrace that moment and **YOURSELF** with gratitude, acceptance, and **unconditional** love, **THEN** you will be a powerful agent of **PEACE** and **COMPASSION** in our world.

22

–Carole

One word of advice, or piece of wisdom, gained over 80 years of living is simply…

To build a strong, personal relationship with Jesus Christ.

It took me 70 years to discover the value of this, but it changed my life for the good. You can do this by talking to Jesus every day about anything that comes to mind. You can pray (thanks and praise); you can read scripture and anything else that will help you in this endeavor. I have found the books by Sarah Young a great help. I am a happier, more productive disciple of Christ for doing this.

-Charlie

"There is no greater agony than bearing an untold story inside of you."

-Maya Angelou

"We're all just walking each other home."

-Ram Dass

Live your life as though it's half full and not half empty.

-Cheryl

LESSONS LEARNED:

 Know thyself.

 Be true to thyself.

Humility and acceptance. Know that as we are one of six and a half billion people on the earth, we will experience the joys and sorrows of the human condition.

Believe in the power of perseverance.

The power of one. Believe in the possibility of leaving the world a little better for one's passage.

Never cry over spilt milk. Never borrow trouble from tomorrow.

-Chuck

In my work I have often had meetings with communities that are suspicious of an outsider's interest in their cultural heritage. Before one such meeting in India several years ago, I was praying about how best to approach them. Instead of coming up with a pitch, I found myself pondering three words that were telling me how I should be in that difficult meeting:

HUMBLE, TRANSPARENT, KIND.

Those three words have continued to be my mantra in various situations, both high-stake and ordinary. I am by no means always, or even often, able to inhabit that space when I'm dealing with someone, but it's still my go-to. I suppose it's another way of saying be of Christ, meeting Christ. The Rule of St. Benedict talks a lot about seeing Christ in the other, but of course we all have Christ in us.

-Columba

Having spent my whole
entire life wondering
what was wrong with me
and why I wasn't like ev-
eryone else, I recently
learned of Enneagrams,
a peronality test.

Now I know,
there is nothing wrong
with me, I am just a 5.

Know thyself.

~Connie

Lou Holtz is known for his many pithy and meaningful quotes, including:

"I think everybody needs four things in life. Everybody needs something to do, regardless of age. Everybody needs someone to love. Everybody needs something to hope for. And of course, everybody needs something to believe in."

I would supplement these four ideas with:

Everybody needs something to do that is challenging and gratifying.

Everybody needs someone to love, family or friend, and to let them know of your love.

Everybody needs something to hope for, and to seek, for yourself and others.

Everybody needs something to believe in, a personal faith, a creed, a future to look forward to.

~Dale

"I wish I could show you, when you are lonely or in darkness, the astonishing light of your own being."

—Hafiz

One idea, above all others, is bookended by the prose of others: Tempted to live life with an outward focus, the teacher within can be so elusive. Imagine the joy—SEIZE the joy—of living in alignment with your deepest conviction!

29

"Be who you were created to be and you will set the world on fire."

—St. Catherine of Sienna

~Danette

"The gift of faith for those of us called to public service is to be unapologetically who we are."

-Tim Kaine.

This quote comes to me now that campaigns for public office have become charades of the public service they imply.

~Dave D.

Life will never cease to challenge each of us with unexpected and unplanned tumultuous events. Sickness, death, deterioration of one's close relationships, and financial hardship are just a few. Far more important than the difficulty itself, will be our response to it.

Acceptance and adaptation to change can create strength and character within us. It can give us wisdom and understanding in a way we could never have had without the experienced hardship. And it helps if we trust that God is there throughout it all, whether or not we feel His presence in the moment.

Even more importantly, at some point in the future, hardship may provide us the opportunity to empathize and help someone else who experiences a similar difficulty!

~Dave G.

The purpose of business is to serve **people**—to serve the customers with good products, the employees with fair wages, the stockholders with profits, and the community through taxes and philanthropy.

-Dave K.

Always remember to toast

success

AND

failure.

Both define our character and how time will remember us. Raising a glass to strife, hardship, and loss is a reminder to keep the will to endure. And when the glass is raised to success, it's a toast of gratitude for our endurance.

Grace is this gift.

Cheers!

-David D.

"I wish I could take language
    And fold it like cool, moist rags.
    I would lay words on your forehead.
    I would wrap words on your wrists.
    'There, there,' my words would say
    Or something better.
    I would ask them to murmur,
    'Hush' and 'Shh, shhh, it's all right.'
    I would ask them to hold you all night.
    I wish I could take language
    And daub and sooth and cool
    Where fever blisters and burns,
    Where fever turns yourself against you.
    I wish I could take language
    And heal the words that were the wounds
    You have no names for."

                            -Julia Cameron

                            ~Davia

The revered poet, Mary Oliver, completes her poem "The Summer Day," with these words:

"Tell me, what is it you plan to do with your one wild and precious life?"

One precious life. Do we realize the magnitude of the gift we have been given? Have we been awakened to how exhilarating life can be? Most important of all, can we summon the courage to take charge of our lives, put away the excuses, and experience that exhilaration? As hard as this may be to accept, if our lives are mundane, we have only ourselves to blame.

-David M.

I just went to the Merriam-Webster Collegiate Dictionary, 11th Edition, and looked up one word which describes *wisdom* perfectly:

GENUINE.

The definition takes up almost two paragraphs, but my favorite part is: "free from hypocrisy or pretense" followed by *authentic*, then that definition follows. How cool is that?!!

~Dean

With God's grace I have learned to live in the present, not in the past, not the future, just this day, and to turn my life over to Christ.

The blessings have been overwhelming. I was given two pieces of advice that I have carried with me through the years:

PUT YOUR TRUST IN THE LORD DAILY.
LET GO OF WORRY.

Most of the things I've worried about have never happened. Those opportunities of growth have carried me through the death of my precious son, two husbands, and dear family members. I pray daily for the Holy Spirit's wisdom to guide me.

-Delphine

Even at some of the worst times in my life, I have had the ability to approach problems while maintaining my sense of humor, as unusual as that may seem. When that ability has been diminished or, rarely, absent, I have recognized that the issue was an even more troubling one than usual, something that I didn't understand fully or one that required deeper thought, and perhaps wisdom from another trusted individual.

38 Being able to see humor in a situation, and laugh, is a way to cope with the most difficult of problems.

-Dick G.

"CULTURE EATS STRATEGY FOR BREAKFAST."
-PETER DRUCKER

39

-Dick M.

I was a hypocrite.

I was raised in a Christian home and I went through the motions of being a Christian. I did the same as an adult. However, during all those years, I never had an intimate relationship with God. I hardly ever prayed and never read the Bible, I was a hypocrite.

I didn't have time for God, but God still had time for me. In January 2011, I learned about a program that was starting at a local church and God compelled me to attend. That session helped me to see the light, to come out of the darkness, to be born again, and to establish a relationship with our Father God in heaven and His son, Jesus Christ.

I was 76 years old, proof positive that it is never too late to be saved.

-Dick P.

There are only two things I have to remember:

There is a Higher Power and I am not it.

~Dick R.

A little while ago, as I walked through an art museum gallery, I was threading my way between exhibits of *The Saint John's Bible* when a sideways glance registered a beckoning flicker of burnished gold on one of the pages on display.

With that momentary shock of truth we experience when we catch sight of our own reflection in the unfamiliar mirror, my eyes were drawn to an image of "The Son of Man" facing the incipit page of the Gospel of Saint John. I was thumped hard in the chest by the power of it—the power of the *other* in it.

It was fashioned by my hands, but surely *another's* power, not mine. I stopped dead in my stride and wept in the knowledge of it. If not mine, who's?

Now, whatever your answer to that question, in that instant I relearned what I must always have known but regularly forget (or fear?). If we offer our gifts and our true, undefended selves to the creative spirit of God, we will never work alone.

~Donald

ITHAKA
(condensed version)
Constantine P. Cavafy

When you set out for Ithaka
ask that your way be long,
full of adventure, full of instruction.

At many a Summer dawn to enter
with what gratitude, what joy—
ports seem for the first time;
to stop the Phoenician trading centres,
and to buy good merchandise,
mother of pearl and coral, amber and ebony,
to visit many Egyptian cities,
to gather stores of knowledge from the learned.

43

Have Ithaka always in your mind.
Your arrival there is what you are destined for.
But don't in the least hurry the journey.
Better it last for years,
so that when you reach the island you are old,
rich with all you have gained on the way,
not expecting Ithaka to give you wealth.
Ithaka gave you a splendid journey.
Without her you would not have set out.
She hasn't anything else to give you.

And if you find her poor, Ithaka hasn't deceived you.
So wise you have become, of such experience,
that already you'll have understood what these
Ithakas mean.

–Dorothy

IF YOU DON'T SHOW UP YOU DON'T GET TO PLAY THE GAME.

44

It's the best reason in the world to get up each morning!

~Eric H.

There are no expiration dates on long, treasured friendships, nor will there ever be. After all, aren't these the true wealth we earn in life?

45

-Eric M

Disciplines of Customer (and Personal) Interface:

- Defuse hostility. Always establish rapport.
- Depersonalize the issues.
- Understand the problem from the customer's perspective.
- Work on win-win solutions.
- Focus on the big picture.
- Manage the relationship as well as the transaction.
- Always follow-up.

~Faheem

As an end-of-life-chaplain, the wisdom I've learned is:

Do what you love, with whom you love, now and for the rest of your days. It is the only way I know to live well and then die well. No regrets, no worry, just love.

47

-Frank

Stay hopeful and curious. To discard hope leads to despair. To set curiosity aside leads to darkness and inertia. I am hopeful because there is always more to know and the human race is incredibly resilient.

-Fred K.

Whatever you practice, you will get good at.

Practice *listening* and you
will become a good *listener*.

Practice *lying* and you
will get good at *lying*.

Practice *kindness* and you
will get good at *kindness*.

Practice *self-discipline* and you
will become *self-disciplined*.

Decide what you want to be good at, and seek out the opportunities, however small, to practice. This suggests that every day you will make many very small decisions. They are important because they give you a chance to practice good decision making.

-Fred S.

The most effective
antidote to worry
and stress is shifting
the focus to carrying
burdens for and
providing support to
o t h e r s .

~Gary

Be open, listen well, speak kindly and be grateful for your blessings. 51

~Gene

Make interruptions your purpose (or your job). If you are busy with some tasks, and the phone rings or there is someone at your door, make that interruption your job. The person on the phone or at the door will be welcomed and received (much like St. Benedict exhorts his monks to do in receiving guests and strangers as Christ). If I'm at my desk working feverishly on an email (let's say to you) and I hear the church bells ringing, calling me to prayer, it is the interruption that calls me into a direct relationship with God. Even when I'm on a roll at my desk writing a wonderful email and would prefer not to be interrupted, the interruption is like the blank space between stanzas in a poem, or the rest stops in a piece of music. These define what we are about, and will make a big difference in how we approach life.

-Geoffrey

Every breath you take, every step you take is a gift from God.

53

~Gerrie

Keep your mind and heart open to the needs of others.

-Harlan

Life only has meaning if you have people in your life whom you deeply love and deeply love you. Nothing is more important than mat- tering to someone else.

~Harvey

For many folks, north Arkansas may be as close to heaven as they get, for others it's a foretaste of God's future plans for those who believe in Jesus. Let's Go Fish!

-Jack C.

Serenity Prayer

—Reinhold Niebuhr

God grant me the serenity to accept the things I cannot change, courage to change the things I can, and wisdom to know the difference.

Living one day at a time, enjoying one moment at a time; accepting hardships as the pathway to peace, taking as He did, this sinful world as it is, not as I would have it, trusting that He will make all right if I surrender to his will; that I may be reasonably happy in this life and supremely happy with Him forever in the next.

Amen

~Jack S.

I may not be able to control what is going on around me, but I can hold my own.

I find those words to be affirming in this chaotic time.

~Jane B.

I want to share one of my favorite paintings. It is part of the far right panel of the *Isenheim Alterpiece* by Matthias Grunewald, painted in 1510. For the past few years, a copy has been hanging near my prayer chair in my bedroom. There is something about this picture that inspires me as I gaze at it before I launch into the world every morning. This resurrected Jesus is bursting with energy and power. You can feel it if you stay long enough with the image. In my little devotional, *God Calling*, a line caught my eye that describes this painting perfectly, "unlimited power to bless others." This has been my mantra for the last few months. This idea, coupled with this image, gives me the fuel I need to go out into the world to be a blessing to others.

-Jane C.

" Love who you love
With all that you have
And don't waste the time
that flies so fast
Love who you love
And say that you do
Hold on as tight as they'll
let you
Love who you love **"**

–Rascal Flatts

~Jason

60

"Integrity in the ruler is the secret of the wellbeing in the subjects."

61

-St. Leo the Great

~Jeff

Every morning when I get up, I start my day by saying, **"How do I help great people do great things today?"**

Over the years this has helped me create environments of total trust for every person I interacted with, resulting in truly outstanding organizations, both for profit and nonprofit. It is a wonderful joy to see people from all over the world thrive and strive to do ever better.

~Jerre

The universe is one enormous energy field. Energy cannot be created or destroyed. Everything is energy. Thought is energy. What we dwell on grows. If we dwell on joy, joy grows. If we dwell on fear, fear grows. Each of us chooses the quality of our own lives by the thoughts we choose to dwell on. It's that simple and that challenging. No one is to blame, no one to point fingers at. No parent, no Pope, no President, I alone **choose** the quality of my life. I cannot always control my knee-jerk reactions to people and events, but once I become aware of what I am thinking or feeling, then I can intervene. It is then I can **choose** the thought or feeling that I want to grow in my life. Isn't that what freedom is?

~Jerry Ha

Keep in mind that every desire, want, or urge is not automatically a right. Experience teaches us that to be successful in business or life one has to be prepared, work hard, and have the courage to fail and learn from it. Challenges are inherent; alternatively they often lead to new ways of doing things and new things to do... to opportunities. But don't be consumed by success. It brings obligations, not just opportunities. Strive to identify what's truly important and what one has to know to be a decent and productive human being and citizen.

~Jerry Ho

I went to the Bible, to
Proverbs 4, verse 5:

"ACQUIRE WISDOM! ACQUIRE
UNDERSTANDING! DO NOT FOR-
GET NOR TURN AWAY FROM
THE WORDS OF MY MOUTH."

As a Christian, I firmly believe
this underpins my life!

~Jerry J.

Always be supportive of family, friends, and those less fortunate than you, and love your neighbor as yourself.

66

What more to life is there?

~Jerry N

"Father, I desire that they also, whom thou hast given me, may be with me where I am, to behold my glory which thou hast given me in thy love for me before the foundation of the world. O righteous Father, the world has not known thee, but I have known thee, and these know that thou hast sent me. I made known to them thy name, and I will make it known, that the love with which thou hast loved me may be in them and I in them."

John 17:24-2

-Jim B.

Three bits of wisdom I use:

🐦Be yourself

🐦"Patience young grasshopper" (from TV series *Kung Fu)*

🐦"The place God calls you is the place where your deep gladness and the world's deep hunger meet."

-Frederick Buechner

~Jim R.

In the end, when all is said and done, all that really matters are our relationships with God, with our family, our friends and colleagues, and with the poor and disenfranchised, and to be able to answer positively when asked: were we kind, forgiving, and generous with what we had?

~Jim S.

While taking the high road may seem selfless and magnanimous, I also find it much less stressful. Conversely, the more I think about "what's in it for me?" the more anxious I become.

Maybe Catholic guilt is not all that bad?

~Jim T.

As a young girl, I was taught to respect others and treat other people as I would like to be treated myself. And, always try to keep my sense of humor throughout my life as I age.

~Jo

(Note: Jo died at age 89, while this book was being compiled. She kept her sense of humor until the end.)

"When in doubt, do without." This advice was given to me by my dearest friend, sadly now departed, whenever she saw me hesitating over a decision, big or small. I never once regretted heeding those words. I still hear her saying them in times of indecision.

"Shut up and take the ring." My mother's words to me when I told her I didn't want my then-fiance' to spend money on an engagement ring. Her reasoning—it was important to him that I have it. So I shut up and took the ring. Nearly 38 years later I still have it, love it, and cherish it. I always think of her words when someone wants to do something nice for me or give me a gift out of the blue. Often those items or deeds are just as much gifts to the giver as they are to the receiver. To accept graciously and enthusiastically is a gift in return.

~Jo~Ann

My dad had two sayings that he lived by. The first was:

"It's not what you know but who you know."

I fought that saying well into my twenties when it was clear to me that having connections to the "right" people does give you a leg up in life.

The second was:

"As I get older, the less I know."

Now, as I turned 60 years old and have been a judge for 20 years, I do know less and less as time passes. My life is blessed.

-Jodi

"Always doubt your certainty."
Perhaps that is the key for me in living, growing, and loving life. I have found that curiosity keeps me un-hooked in a world that is filled with fundamentalist thinking. It is curiosity that reminds me at a deep level that I do not know it all. Who wants to be around know-it-alls anyway? When one truly embraces curiosity, one becomes open to our human need to be in relationship. Without curiosity, our dialogues become monologues. This sows the seeds of loneliness and unhappiness in the lives of people.

Sadly in these current times, we see people both young and old more and more sure of their righteousness on just about everything. This arrogance does little but alienate people from one another and unravel the fabric of a vibrant, diverse, and rich community.

-Joe C.

Believe in a higher power,
family, friends, and trust.
Be prepared to deal with
disappointment.
But, continue to trust.

~Joe M.

A few years back, I told a dear friend that I was tired of losing out for someone else to win; tired of compromising something for the good of someone else. He taught me love benefits all mutually, and that in fact, because I *am* love, I benefit all whom I come in contact with. When I told him of a mistake I had made, he told me that love makes no mistakes, and that perfect love casts out all fear of mistakes. With his guidance, I changed my attitude and my life for good. As the Bible teaches: "Now abideth Faith, Hope, and Charity, the greatest of these being Love."

~Joe W.

Desire is always stronger than satisfaction. Therefore true satisfaction can only be achieved by being grateful to God for what you already have.

-John and Kathy

"MUCH IS REQUIRED FROM THOSE WHOM MUCH IS GIVEN, AND MUCH MORE IS REQUIRED FROM THOSE TO WHOM MUCH MORE IS GIVEN."

This Bible passage defines my focus and priorities. I am Blessed that my wife and children (including sons-in-law) also believe strongly in this passage, it being a guiding light in their lives. It encompasses how we spend our time, how we use our talents wisely to help others and how we share our material possessions to make a difference. My parents exemplified the importance of this when I was growing up. The power of compelling examples is very real.

-John B.

I am confident the two most important words in the English language are:

Common

and

Sense.

79

Conrad Hilton had many note-worthy and insightful quotes but my favorite is still:

"Remember to tuck the shower curtain inside the bathtub."

~John D.

SHOW UP.
FILL UP.
STAND UP.

I see this applying to much of life. Not much happens if we do not **SHOW UP**, for example, at the family gathering, church, voting booth, class, social gathering. Showing up is more than a physical presence. It means being present mentally, emotionally, spiritually, and ready to participate.

FILL UP means drinking in, absorbing, and consuming whatever is offered.

STAND UP is doing something with what has been received, taking whatever has been the blessing, and making the world a better place.

~John F.

As abbot, I have learned the hard way the importance of taking counsel from the community. At first, I didn't know how to do this when the community was oriented in a direction that would result in a misalignment with the local bishop. Saint Benedict, in his wisdom, instructs the abbot to lead in such a manner that the community cannot engage in justifiable grumbling. In community, if one looks around, there will always be reasons for grumblings, the abbot has to make sure that he does not contribute to that pile!

~John K.

Wisdom is powerful,

82 *but only when shared.*

~John L.

We are to listen for the beat of the Sacred deep within all things. It is the heartbeat of God. ⁸³ This is our only hope.

-John P. N.

When we take care of each other, everything else seems to take care of itself.

-John R.

As you climb life's ladder of success, treat everyone with respect and a smile. You will probably meet them on the way back down.

-John S.

"Making the simple complicated is commonplace; making the complicated simple, awesomely simple, that's creativity."

-Charles Mingus

    Mingus's point here has universal application. In the arts, in science, in business and even in personal interaction, those who are able to put an idea or a concept into an elegant nutshell are usually the persons who I admire the most.

-John W.

In my youth, I wondered why classmates, friends, parents, and scout leaders often surprised me with comments or decisions I didn't expect. Later, when I began selling things, these unexpected answers became more frequent and equally confusing. Then I met a wise and experienced sales manager who provided the following insight that has guided my interactions ever since. Perhaps not profound but certainly interesting:

"Never be surprised when people act as people."

−Jon

Better to want something you never had, than to have something you never wanted.

-Judy and Lee

If service is beneath you,
then
leadership is beyond you. *89*

-Karel

KINDNESS SPOKEN HERE

I had these simple words framed and hanging in the bell room of the church for adults and children alike to see. I have it now in the music office to remind me of why I serve through music. I think kindness above all else is what I feel God is asking of me.

-Karmen

Servant Leadership is "All about YOU."

It's being the Water Carrier for those who pledge to get their jobs done. It's taking responsibility when things go wrong, and giving credit to others when things go right— with TRUST being the bedrock of the organization's culture.

-Ken

91

Always tell the truth—it is so hard to remember the lies.

~Kent E.

I am the grandpa that lives in "the age of technology." When my grandchildren and I are together, they don't use their cell phones, video games, or iPads. We barely have the TV on (except Tom and Jerry cartoons before they go to sleep). We play in the yard, we bake and cook, we talk, walk in the park, work the garden, feed the birds and we love to look for "special" rocks. We take trips, catch bugs and frogs, and simply enjoy each other. We look for the marvel in everyday life.

~Kent L.

"For I know the plans I have for you, declares the Lord, plans to prosper you and not to harm you. Plans to give you hope and a future."
—Jeremiah 29:11

-Kerry

"Purpose becomes purposeful when it touches and enriches the lives of others"

A Bonus: "No amount of *what* or *how* can ever compensate for a lack of *why*."

~Kevin C.

This simple prayer has been like a balm to me for over two decades:

"God grant me the serenity to accept the things I cannot change, courage to change the things I can, and wisdom to know the difference."

While often associated with Alcoholics Anonymous, where I first came across it, the prayer was written, I believe, by American theologian Reinhold Niebuhr.

~Kevin L

I've dealt with worry most of my life. When I surrendered my life to Jesus, I felt peace for the first time. I'm not sure whether it was out of pure gratitude, or my personal desire, but when I'm able to fully trust in Jesus, I'm more at peace and things seem to work out.

~Larry

You will never
regret doing
acts of kindness.

~LaVonne

We think that our guiding light changes over time and depends on what stage of life we're in. For instance, at this stage, we are in the process of selling our home. With that decision comes downsizing and decluttering.

Another example and more permanent guiding principle: our four grandchildren, ages 10-15, are very well taken care of. With that in mind, we have decided that all Christmas and birthday gifts will be money they cannot keep. They must give it away. They have formed what they call the "Cousins Council," and have found which charities speak to their hearts.

In each envelope, each year, we include the words of John Wesley:

"Do all the good you can, in all the ways you can, in all the places you can, at all the times you can, to all the people you can, as long as ever you can."

~Leone and Vin

Two Wolves

One evening an old man told his grandson about a battle that goes on within people. He said, "My son, the battle is between two wolves inside us all. One is Evil. It is anger, envy, jealousy, sorrow, regret, greed, arrogance, self-pity, guilt, resentment, inferiority, lies, false pride, superiority, and ego.

The other is Good. It is joy, peace, love, hope, serenity, humility, kindness, benevolence, empathy, generosity, truth, compassion, and faith."

The grandson thought about it for a minute and then asked his grandfather: "Which wolf wins?"

The old man simply replied, "The one you feed."

–Author unknown

~Linda W.

❖A window in time should be explored for the sublime.

❖Know yourself, then consider your "possibles."

❖When living provides a "window," use it.

❖When presented with two doors, open both and peek through.

~Mark N.

102 ZIPPITY!

~Mark R.

A strong faith, close-knit family, and dear friends are vital in helping a person cope during difficult times.

-Mark Y.

Years ago, I used to fret over bad things that happened to me. Later I would look back and realize that an opportunity had presented itself as a result. I now believe: "All things for a reason." The reason won't necessarily be immediately apparent, but it helps to focus on the paths and choices the incident presents.

-Mary H.

LOVE is the first word that came to my mind. We all know that expressing and feeling the love that God has blessed us with is the most powerful warmth to our hearts, minds, and bodies.

Thoughtful and heartfelt communication throughout our ages from childhood to now is so important for each of us. The communication we give and receive in our lives keeps us close to one another, both in our families and in our friendships. The stories that come from this communication is what life is all about.

–Mary Joy

"The real voyage of discovery in life consists not in seeking new landscapes but in having new eyes."

–Marcel Proust

~Mary L.

"Our deepest fear is not that we are inadequate. Our deepest fear is that we are powerful beyond measure. It is the light, not our darkness that most frightens us. We ask ourselves, 'Who am I to be brilliant, gorgeous, talented, fabulous?' Actually, who are you not to be? You are a child of God. Your playing small does not serve the world. There is nothing enlightened about shrinking so that other people won't feel insecure around you. We are all meant to shine, as children do. We were born to make manifest the glory of God that is within us. It's not just in some of us; it's in everyone. And as we let our own light shine, we unconsciously give other people permission to do the same. As we are liberated from our own fear, our presence automatically liberates others."
–Marianne Williamson

-Mary Lynn

Some years ago I read the book *Tuesdays with Morrie*, which impacted my life significantly. On his deathbed Morrie belatedly came to realize the deep significance of the important people in his life. Since then I have read the remarks of a hospice nurse who charted her experiences with patients in their last moments. She found that it is not money or status that held true importance for them, rather it was the significance of relationships in their lives and often, the deep regrets about not giving these relationships the time and effort that they deserved. Relationships enrich our lives to such a great degree that I don't want to experience regrets but will work to take advantage of the treasure while I can.

~Mary Rita

Listen.

This first word of the Rule of Saint Benedict seems to me the source and summit of wisdom. Listen with the ear of the heart. Listen to God in Scripture, in the embrace of those who love you and lift you up. Listen to God in those who challenge you, calling you to be a truer image of the Christ you bear. Listen to the God in the suffering, calling you to see the Christ they bear. Listen to God in your uniquely gifted self. Treasure your gifts but do not hoard them, for it is through your particular gifts that the world most clearly hears the voice of God.

-Mary S.

The Abbot asked me,
"What do you seek?"

I respoded, "I seek the
mercy of God, and
fellowship in this
community."

I figure if I seek these two things
(or are they really one?), I will be
seeking what is good, meaningful,
challenging, and joyful in my life.

-Michael

We'll See

At the end of the movie *Charlie Wilson's War*, a CIA officer, played by Philip Seymour Hoffman, makes a point by telling the story of a Zen Master. He observes the people of his village celebrating a young boy's new horse as a wonderful gift. "We'll see," the Zen Master says. When the boy falls off the horse and breaks his leg, everyone says the horse is a curse. "We'll see," says the Master. Then war breaks out, the boy cannot be conscripted because of his injury, and everyone says the horse was a fortunate gift. "We'll see," the master says again.

~Mike and Linda

Success is attained and earned through the process of searching for "elegant solutions" (i.e. best possible solutions considering the most relevant variables), by encouraging and engaging everyone in a win/win, positive atmosphere/culture, and by celebrating and sharing the results. This philosophy applies to both organizations and families.

-Mike E.

What leadership attribute
is most important?

This is the question I often ask others as I'm seeking to understand leadership. It seemed that the consensus was the ability to use good judgment. If the leader has all the other leadership attributes, but for whatever reason chooses the wrong answer or direction, much or all is lost. This certainly puts the weight on the *what* versus the *how* of decision making. However, recent times have caused some rethinking of that, for while getting it right does matter, the how matters too.

My hope is that we see more leaders in the future who care about both winning and how they win, that demonstrate good judgment, but also integrity, compassion, grace, a little humility, and I hope we see more leaders like Lincoln and Churchill.

~Mike H.

I feel my generation (baby boomers) is so blessed to live in the age that we have. We have experienced so many marvels... from firsts in space, the advent of technologies, and increased quality of life. However, these advances have not come without a price, especially to our environment. Addressing global warming is the most serious issue facing us and future generations. Without constructive world action and cooperation, the health and welfare of the planet and its occupants are on a perilous path. Let us all work towards worldly solutions to this huge problem. We are all in this together.

-Mike N.

Whenever possible, wait to send any letter or communication that includes even limited emotion. Write it and edit it. Then wait. Whether a professional letter or personal note, if the situation is one where you are the least bit likely to regret what you have said, take that possibility out of the equation by exercising the wisdom of discernment.

Wait at least a day and reread your words. Few situations call for immediate responses—especially those for which written communication is best. Efficiency of response can be reckless. Take your time. Be sure you are saying what you want to say and no more.

-Mike O.

Years ago I asked my mother why she did not have gray hair at the age of 80. She said,

"You cannot worry about things you have no control over. That wasted energy causes worry lines and gray hair."

I live by that advice and find my life is positive and satisfying.

~Mimi

As the second oldest of ten children, I, along with my older sister, would be responsible to help clean the house with Mom every Saturday morning before we could go out and play or to a matinee movie. I would rush through and invariably Mom would check our work and point out something I missed and I would have to redo it under her supervision. She would remind me that I should do it properly the first time and offer it up to the Lord. I was paging through a daily devotion flip card and found it:

Colossians 3:23: "Whatever you do, do your work Heartily, as for the Lord rather than for men."

I no longer clean my house, but I try to do any task the right way the first time, and when it is one I do not like doing, I do it for the Lord.

~Nancy

"Be generous."

Be generous with your family, your friends, yourself, and your God. Give freely of your time, your praise, your devotion, your love, your patience, your treasure. Share your dreams, gratitude and hopes. Listen to others with your ears and your heart when they share themselves with you. Protect the helpless and homeless as best you can. Talk to God every day.

-Paddy

Taking advantage of positive and fun opportunities when they are presented, rather than waiting for the perfect time, avoids missed opportunities.

-Pat

A few things that came to my mind...

I think a lot about how grateful I am for this beautiful earth and how fortunate we are to walk a land filled with trees, flowers, birds, skies and stars, streams and mountains and so many wondrous animals. I hope we find some ways to preserve it for those who come after us.

I've long been a fan of John Stewart, he of the old Kingston Trio. In one of his songs he had the line, "They were just a lot of people doing the best they could." I can't tell you how many times I've thought of that line. It's so easy to get judgmental and question the acts and motives of others. But it seems wise to remember that most people are doing the best they can with the cards they have been dealt.

What if I started living as though everything was going to be okay?

~Patty

Follow the universal
laws of *Love*:

- Love yourself.

- Love your neighbor.

- Love your family, even if you don't agree with them on all things.

121

- Love your community, love your country, love the world.

- Return no evil for evil.

- Turn the other cheek.

- Love God.

-Paul H.

Just be yourself. You cannot be anyone else, and who you are *is enough.*

~Paul K.

You have my complete attention.

In all manner of relationships—colleague, partner, family, community—we are asked by others to listen carefully. But attentive and empathetic listening is hard to do well, because our egos get in the way.

To give our complete attention is an act of both hospitality and humility involving more than simply welcoming another person. It means being present, perhaps offering refreshments or a place to rest, and always an open ear.

123

Giving real priority to someone requires active engagement with their words—hearing, acknowledging, asking questions, affirming. The longer we know someone, the greater the need to consciously practice listening, lest we come to think we've heard it all before and slowly stop hearing. When we listen carefully we lay the foundation for trust even when we don't see eye to eye.

~Peter

As a student for many years of the art and science of training and performance at work, I think Peter Drucker's philosophy on knowledge continues to sum it up:

"We now accept the fact that learning is a lifelong process of keeping abreast of change. And the most pressing task is to teach people how to learn. The essence of management is to make knowledge productive. Knowledge exists only in application. (Actionable knowledge as opposed to just information.) We will not be limited by the information we have. We will be limited by our ability to process that information."
–Peter Drucker

-Phil J.

Lucky is the person who can find a true passion in their life. When one has, they should take this passion, run with it for all they are worth, but never, ever compromise their values and principles. Finding my life's passion and running with it is what made me a happy fulfilled person.

~Phil T.

Growing up in South America, it never occurred to me that I would end up in the USA and become a citizen of another country; going to New York City—never, seeing Mount Rushmore—impossible, marrying an American man—too far fetched to consider!

Here I am.

God had other plans for me and I had to adapt to another way of life, learn to speak another language and to drive a car.

Who knew? God knew.

To a certain extent, I have done the unattainable. God has many ways to teach us lessons. So do not discount God's plans. God had many ways to show another path. I have embraced and loved my new country and new experiences and I'm waiting to learn what else God has in store for me.

-Rebeca

SOMETIMES GOD LETS YOU HIT BOTTOM SO YOU WILL DISCOVER HE IS the rock AT THE BOTTOM.

~Renee

I have found in my 74 years that God presents us with many possibilities in life.

"Opportunities are like garage sales, there is one around every corner. You just have to watch for the signs."

My father had a favorite saying about being willing to try something new and sometimes not succeeding:

Show me a ball player who doesn't make errors and I'll show you someone who doesn't try for the ball.

He also taught me to :

"Never forget those who help you in life and never worry about those who wrong you."

-Richard C.

At the heart of living a purposeful life is the call to unlock our gifts.
Unlocking means:

Gifts
+ Passions
+ Values
_____
Our Calling.

Each of us is an experiment
of one. There are no one-size-fits-all
ways to live life. Each of us is called
to choose our own way, regardless of
the crucibles we find ourselves facing.

Purpose matters; our most human need is to find and fulfill meaning in our lives. The way to find and
fulfill meaning is to wake up, on purpose, every single day and answer
the call to make a difference in just
one person's life that day.

The call to make a difference
never ceases up to our last moment,
up to our last breath.

-Richard L.

THE PATH TO HAPPINESS

For me, the first path to happiness is *gratitude*. A life of gratefulness begins with the realization that life is a gift and a blessing. Nothing is guaranteed; the world doesn't owe us anything. Everything is to be cherished. In the infinite wisdom of Rabbi Abraham Joshua Heschel: "Just to be is a blessing. Just to live is holy."

The second path to happiness is *service*. Shortly after college I joined a volunteer program in Colorado. On my bedroom wall I hung a Maryknoll poster with the following words from the Indian writer Rabindranath Tagore: "I slept and dreamt that life was joy. I awoke and found that life was service. I served and behold, service was joy." My yearning to serve comes from my mom. She lived her life for others.

The third path to happiness is *purpose*. My dear friend Br. Dietrich Reinhart (deceased), who served as the long-time President of Saint John's University, was fond of the following quotation from Frederick Buechner: "The place God calls you is where your deep gladness and the world's deep hunger meet." Truer words have seldom been spoken.

~Rob

May I be patient, gentle, kind, and honest with myself and others, and may I do my best to exercise these simple principles in every step I take, every thought I think, and every word I speak.

131

~Roger

"I defy description. My self is full of contradictions, shadings, changes, inconsistencies, and subtleties. Labels can be useful, but they don't define me. I can't be put into a neat little box. Spilling out, I move with the cosmos. My being consists of millions of molecules keeping time to the rhythm of the universe. Today I embrace all of whom I am, including the parts I don't yet understand. Looking forward to the surprises of my blossoming personhood, I am grateful for the complicated and sacred me.

–Eleanor Ruth Wagner

-Ron

132

Being grateful
is an invitation
to turn life's
ordinary

moments into
extraordinary
ones.

-Sheri

Practice the art of delicious conversation—sharing your heart and listening to others. Practice true presence to another like it's the most important muscle in your body. Notice what throws you off from connection and gentle ways to get back on track. Rumi captures this beautifully:

"Your task is not to seek for love, but merely to seek and find all the barriers within yourself that you have built against it."

All of this being-human is made more tolerable by delighting in our bodies, laughing often, breathing in the outdoors, digging in the dirt, and having soft fur and skin to snuggle with.

-Sherry E.

What may seem to be so, may not be so.

So how do you find out the truth? You must be clear about your own truth, and then ask for the other person's truth. This can be a fearful thing so I try to go to Eleanor Roosevelt's words about conquering fear:

"The only way to conquer your fear is to do the very thing you are afraid of."

-Sherry S.

If we can call the future "the future" we should be able to call the past "the pasture." We really can do nothing about the future because it is always just out of reach, and if we spend almost any time in the pasture we will only step in shit. We only have now, so make the most of what is right at hand and savor what you have now in "the present."

-Shoebob

Be kind, loving, and caring to all and you will have a fulfilling life. [137]

-Steve G.

Gratitude

Every day that goes by I find myself more and more grateful for darn near everything in my life—family, friends, and fruitful work for starters. I am also grateful for my country, my home, and my physical and financial well being. In truth, the list is so long it can overwhelm me at times. The older I get (now 67), the more emotional I get thinking about how fortunate I am.

Grace and gratitude are both derived from the Latin, *gratus*, meaning pleasing or thankful. I think gratitude helps keep one self-aware, humble, and other-focused. Maybe it even leads to grace, or so I hope. So the wisdom, if you will, is

BE GRATEFUL. IT AFFECTS EVERYTHING.

~Steve H.

In these challenging times, I find this prayer especially meaningful.

Lord, make me an instrument of your peace
Where there is hatred let me sow love
Where there is injury, pardon
Where there is doubt, faith
Where there is despair, hope
Where there is darkness, light
Where there is sadness, joy
O divine master, grant that I may
Not so much seek to be consoled as to console
To be understood as to understand
To be loved as to love
For it is in giving that we receive
It is in pardoning that we are pardoned
And it is in dying that we are born to
eternal life. Amen
—St. Francis of Assisi

In reciting this prayer, I'm acknowledging the gulf between intention and practice and I'm encouraged by the results I've experienced. Very concretely, I've focused on being a better listener.

~Susan

Believe in yourself & have fun.

140

~Tess C.

Illegitimi non carborundum
Don't let the bastards get you down!

When all still seems lost I recite this psalm:
"I AM CONFIDENT OF THIS; I WILL SEE
THE GOODNESS OF THE LORD IN THE
LAND OF THE LIVING. WAIT FOR THE
LORD, BE STRONG. TAKE HEART AND
WAIT FOR THE LORD."

141

And I remember what Mr. Fred Rogers says:
"Look for the Helpers."

-Tess R.

Tuskegee Red Tail Squadron
Guiding Principles:

Aim High
Believe in Yourself

142

Use Your Brain
Never Quit
Be Ready to Go
Expect to Win

-Tim B.

Play the hand you are dealt with grace, passion, and courage.

If you get knocked down, pick yourself up with a smile and give it another whack, this time with commitment.

But don't take yourself too damn seriously.

And don't judge the journeys of others.

You don't know what **you don't know.**

Spend everyday enjoying the gift of your special journey.

-Tim M.

I think many of us learned a lot about who we are and what we had accomplished in the Great Recession. I'm lucky to have recovered and ended ahead of where I was originally. I now believe luck is highly under credited, both good and bad luck.

-Tom La

Everything is connected with Jesus at the center.

I try to live that connectedness by remembering my days growing up on the farm. No rain, no crops. No sun, no growth, and vice versa. With the rain things grew. With the sun things flourished. The death of an animal, an accident, the weather, could have a profound impact on us. We would pray for God's help and guidance. I try to bring this into my priesthood believing that we are all connected, that we are on this journey together as a people and as a world. Whatever we do, including the simplest things, does have an effect on everyone and everything.

-Tom Lo

145

Jesus loves you.
To know that He is sharing
your walk is comforting,
especially during dark times.

-Tom M.

Plan with steps and targets. Live by design, not default. It's never too late to start planning.

Collect **contacts**. Serve and honor them. Mentor them. Be nice to them.

Be an avid **listener**. Be a devoted student and practitioner of the art of listening.

Perseverance. The main thing is to... keep the main thing. Don't sweat the little things, they belong in your "f*** it bucket."

No matter what, enjoy the journey.

~Tom N.

"The privilege of a lifetime is being who you are."

–Joseph Campbell

8

So, live a truthful life and help others do the same.

~Tom W.

I would say my personal piece of wisdom came from when I got locked up. I had time to look back on the past and see the things that caused me to be put in prison. I feel if I wouldn't have been put in there, I would still be drinking and doing drugs, and that was the cause of all my problems, troubles, and downfalls. So I would say to all, always think and always ask God to guide you before you let alcohol, drugs, or whatever it may be blind you from living your life with good judgment, knowledge, and for God. We do have choices. Ask God to lead you in the right way, and do good for others.

-Tony H.

As part of my "journey of discovery" at 50, I worked with a life coach who walked me through several exercises to craft what she called my own personal Dharma code. Here it is: "Live deliberately a life of meaning, spiritual awareness, service to others, creative pursuits, and everyday accomplishments that reinforce all things good about myself, humanity, and where the two intersect." I carry this around in my wallet, have it memorized and placed around the house. I don't think I have fulfilled it yet, but I am on my way. I came to it as a personal guide for myself.

-Tony K.

My early life was formed by my grandmother, who was also my best friend growing up. From her came my belief and practice that when I help people to become happy, then I am happy myself.

-Val

I was once in a small entryway with a group of people, waiting for a door to be unlocked. Someone noticed a bug on the floor. We circled and watched. Nobody knew what kind of bug it was. But we marveled at its apparent sense of purpose, its determination and energy, its refusal to be daunted by the distance it needed to cover. There were expressions of awe, admiration, and appreciation from the group of people.

When the door was unlocked and people filed inside, several said how glad they were that they had the opportunity to watch the bug. An older man hung back, so he could be the last to go inside. And when he thought no one was looking, he stepped on the bug.

Every life has meaning, value, and purpose, even if we don't understand it—a purpose just as important as mine.

~Warren H.

Integrity

first and above all.

Develop a work ethic from a young age, along with respect for all. 153

Be polite and humble
always.

Persistence is key to success, just after integrity.

~Warren S.

Many years ago, my friend Dick and I were presenting a weekend retreat, Friday to Sunday, for parishioners at a retreat house in Farmington, Minnesota. Near the end of our last session on Sunday, Dick said that he and I had given them all the wisdom we had and asked the participants to share their wisdom with us. "Tell us what you learned in your lifetime," Dick said. Among those who shared their wisdom was a small elderly lady, using a walker, who said,

154 *"What I have learned in my life is the exact right thing to say in a given situation... and not to say it."*

~Wayne

To You, my Good and Lovely People:

You gave much; now give more.

You were kind; now be kinder.

You were generous of your time; find
      ways to make your time even more
      available to do good works.

You love; now open your hearts to love
      even more.

You show compassion; be even more
      compassionate.

Love yourself, as God loves you.

Trust and strive to be trusted, for it is the
      bedrock of your very being.

Be open to other's ideas, for they too
      need to be heard.

Be righteous, but do not flaunt it, for it is
      the gift of maturity.

Above all, search your soul for wisdom;
      it is there within you, hidden only
      when you are unsure of yourself

–Anonymous

-Zeke

ACKNOWLEDGMENTS

First and foremost, thank you wise and generous friends for contributing to this book. Because of who you are and your influence on me, you were the "purpose" and only reason this book was created.

My thanks to Curtis and Liz of North Star Press for accepting Vintage Wisdom into your stable of published works. When first introduced to your eclectic facility (with my daughter-in-law Hanna), I knew working with you would be a remarkable experience. And it has. Indeed, you are marvelous and talented professionals. And to Helen, the manuscript's editor, you were delightful to work with. You brought clarity to many of the writings and put up with my endless questions. Thank you.

I thank my children and their spouses (and a certain grandson) for encouraging me in this endeavor and for your understanding in not being asked to participate in the writings. And especially to son Billy, for helping me muddle through the technical aspects of the computer and for your zeal for the project. This meant a lot to me.

My special thanks to Sherry E., who was my first encourager and contributor, and who edited my initial request letter that kicked off the project.

And finally, with enormous gratitude to my wife Teresa, You were my greatest champion in this nine-month process. Your excitement for the project (and for me), spurred me on from the beginning to the book's completion.